To my mom and dad—and to the Eric Huang in an alternate universe who became a proper paleontologist.
E.H.

To my mom Micaela, my love Marine, and the little ones Ivan, Sebastian, Adelita, and Martin. To my dad, wherever he may be. Thanks to both my Argentinian family (David, Sil, Pitu) and French family (Corinne, Jeremy, Marine, Jean-Luc, Nadette) who accompany and support me on this journey.
F.A.

Up Close & Incredible: Dinosaurs © 2025 Quarto Publishing plc.
Text © 2025 Eric Huang. Illustrations © 2025 Facundo Aguirre.

First published in 2025 by Wide Eyed Editions, an imprint of The Quarto Group.
100 Cummings Center, Suite 265D, Beverly, MA 01915, USA.
T +1 978-282-9590 F +1 078-283-2742 **www.Quarto.com**

WTS TAX d.o.o., Žanova ulica 3, 4000 Kranj, Slovenia
www.wts-tax.si

The right of Facundo Aguirre to be identified as the illustrator and Eric Huang to be identified as the author of this work has been asserted by them in accordance with the Copyright, Designs and Patents Act, 1988 (United Kingdom).

All rights reserved.

No part of this publication may be reproduced, stored in a retrieval system, or transmitted, in any form, or by any means, electrical, mechanical, photocopying, recording, or otherwise without the prior written permission of the publisher or a license permitting restricted copying.

ISBN 978-0-7112-8496-8
The illustrations were created digitally
Set in Hipton Sans and Brandon Grotesque

Designer: Myrto Dimitrakoulia
Editor: Lucy Menzies
Production Controller: Robin Boothroyd
Commissioning Editor: Alex Hithersay
Art Director: Karissa Santos
Publisher: Debbie Foy

Manufactured in Shaoguan, China SL042025

9 8 7 6 5 4 3 2 1

UP CLOSE & INCREDIBLE
DINOSAURS

WRITTEN BY **ERIC HUANG**

ILLUSTRATED BY **FACUNDO AGUIRRE**

WIDE EYED EDITIONS

HOW TO USE THIS BOOK

Turn to any page to see a different dinosaur. With each new visit, you'll spot something new! Read the introduction to find out what you're looking at, and discover some fascinating facts. Which herbivore might have had a crest on its head that looked like a party hat? Which creature had a club-shaped tail that it used to smash its predators? And which dino was the size of a turkey?

Next, take your magnifying glass and search for the 10 things to spot. Look closely at each hectic, mischief-filled scene. You'll find hidden gags, hijinks, and lots of surprising facts in every illustration.

When you're done with your tour of the dinosaurs, turn to page 38 to see how big each dinosaur really was. Can you remember where in the book you met them? If not, don't worry! With your trusty magnifying glass, go back for one more adventure. You're sure to spot much more the next time around. On page 40, you'll find a timeline of dino discoveries.

Finally, turn to page 42 to reveal where all the search-and-find details were hiding. How many did you discover?

Well, what are you waiting for? Grab your magnifying glass and get ready to see dinosaurs like you've never seen them before—up close!

Look at the timeline to see when the dino lived.

Meet each dinosaur with need-to-know facts in the introduction.

Use your magnifying glass to look for the 10 things to spot hidden in, on, and around the dinosaur.

This panel shows you how big each creature was compared to a human.

CONTENTS

TOOLS OF THE TRADE
Everything you need to dig for dinosaurs.
8–9

T. REX TEETH
Tyrannosaurus rex
10–11

MOWER-MOUTH
Nigersaurus
12–13

HORN FACE
Triceratops
14–15

CLAWS OUT
Therizinosaurus
16–17

QUITE THE CREST
Parasaurolophus
18–19

KILLER CLAWS
Velociraptor
20–21

WINGING IT
Archaeopteryx
22–23

SPINNING PLATES
Stegosaurus
24–25

WELCOME TO THE CLUB
Ankylosaurus
26–27

A NECK AHEAD
Diplodocus
28–29

SET SAIL!
Spinosaurus
30–31

BONE HEAD
Pachycephalosaurus
32–33

A BIT PRICKLY
Amargasaurus
34–35

A FAN OF FEATHERS
Kulindadromeus
36–37

THE AGE OF DINOSAURS
38–39

TIMELINE OF DISCOVERIES
40–41

ANSWERS
42–43

GLOSSARY & FURTHER READING
44–45

TOOLS OF THE TRADE

Dinosaurs ruled our planet for nearly 200 million years. They evolved into all sorts of **INCREDIBLE** sizes. The smallest were squirrel-sized, while the largest were longer than a blue whale! Travel back in time through the pages of this book, and get **UP CLOSE** to some of the most fascinating and ferocious dinosaurs. Join our team of tiny paleontologists as they examine the teeth, horns, feathers, and armor of different dinosaurs. Hidden throughout the book are ten tools that they use to uncover fossils of these prehistoric creatures. Can you find them?

10 THINGS TO SPOT

1 ROCK HAMMER Fossils, the petrified remains of dinosaurs, are found between layers of rock. Hammers are used to break open the rock to see if anything is inside. This has to be done very carefully or the fossil could be damaged! Chisels are often used for smaller rocks.

2 DENTAL PROBE These aren't just for our teeth! Paleontologists use them to dig out fragile specimens from the matrix, which is the sediment and rock that surrounds fossils. Dental probes are used for the most detailed and careful work.

3 TOOTHBRUSH Another tool for teeth used by paleontologists, toothbrushes are super useful for brushing away excess sediment, dirt, and soil. Paintbrushes and brooms also sweep away unwanted debris from the fossils.

4 SIEVE Some fossils are teeny tiny. They can get lost in the sediment at a dig site. A sieve helps to separate miniature fossils, such as broken pieces of bone, from bits of rock.

5 MAGNIFYING LOUPE These are small magnifying glasses that can fit in your pocket. They allow paleontologists to examine the details of a fossil and decide if something they've found is actually a fossil . . . or just a rock.

6 MEASURING TAPE Everything at a fossil dig is measured and cataloged. Measuring tape is needed to record the dimensions of every fossil, as well as how deep in the rocks it was found.

7 GPS TRACKER The location in which a fossil is found can tell us a lot about its life. Paleontologists use GPS devices and maps to pinpoint exactly where every bone or impression was uncovered. It also helps to remember the location of the dig when you need to return at a later time.

8 ADHESIVE Many fossils are very fragile and can't be removed in the field without being damaged or destroyed. Mild adhesives, or glues, are used to secure fragile specimens so they can survive the trip from a field to the lab.

9 NOTEPAD Paleontologists record almost everything they do in the field. Many carry notepads to describe how a fossil was found and what the team did to remove it from the rocks, as well as any other parts of the day. Diaries of the dig contain important information to reveal a fossil's secrets.

10 CAMERA Along with their notepads, paleontologists use cameras to document a dig. Visual records show the stages of a dig and what a fossil looked like when it was first discovered. Plus, it's handy for a group selfie!

T. REX TEETH

These teeth were made for biting! Their owner, *Tyrannosaurus rex* (pronounced tie-RAN-oh-SOR-us rex), was made for catching prey. The name of this meat-eating dinosaur means "tyrant lizard king." *Tyrannosaurus rex*, *T. rex* for short, was one of the largest predatory dinosaurs ever. It had titanic teeth to match. The largest dinosaur tooth found so far comes from a *T. rex*, which, from root to crown, is taller than a pigeon. An adult had up to sixty teeth in its massive jaws—and several hundred over a lifetime. Similar to sharks, when a *T. rex* lost a tooth, it grew back!

MESOZOIC | Triassic | Jurassic | Cretaceous

SIZE COMPARISON

10 Things to Spot

LETHAL BANANAS The side teeth in a *T. rex*'s mouth were very long. One paleontologist called them "lethal bananas!" Their saw-like edges allowed *T. rex* to slice through the tough skin of its prey.

D FOR DENTAL *T. rex*'s upper front teeth were much smaller than the slicers at the sides. In cross section, they were shaped like a capital "D." This made them strong enough to hold onto struggling prey without breaking.

PACKING A BITE The bite of a *T. rex* had the weight of three small cars! *T. rex* was an ambush predator. It waited for just the right moment to pounce on its prey . . . jaws first.

SLOW DOWN *T. rex* was massive and strong, but it wasn't fast, with a top speed estimated at 10 mph. That's a lot slower than a cheetah or a horse. Most humans could probably out-walk a *T. rex*!

FIGHTING BACK Many dinosaurs on the menu were faster than *T. rex* or small enough to hide. Others had armored bodies, sharp horns, and spiked tails that made every *T. rex* think twice before ordering them for dinner.

LOOK OUT! *T. rex* had excellent vision. Its orange-sized eyes are still the largest of any land animal! Facing forward, set far apart and high on the head, they were able to spot movement from very far away. Tyrannosaurs could likely detect more colors than we can.

SUPER SMELLY The olfactory bulbs are areas in the brain that control smell. *T. rex* had huge ones, which means it had a super-sensitive nose. Like many living animals, *T. rex* may have marked its territory using smells.

LISTEN UP The middle ear bones of a *T. rex* were very long. This is evidence of high-quality hearing, which aided its hunting skills. Scientists believe *T. rex* was very talkative. It likely used low growls to communicate.

ALL GROWN UP A *T. rex* hatchling was about the size of a border collie. Like humans, they had growth spurts in their teens, becoming taller and bulkier. By its twentieth birthday, a *T. rex* was as big as a school bus!

JAZZ HANDS *T. rex* had tiny arms with two fingers. They were too small to help with hunting. Some paleontologists think they may have been used to attract mates. Many birds wave colorful plumes to impress a partner. Maybe *T. rex* arms were brightly colored and used in a similar way, in a Tyrannosaurus tango!

MOWER-MOUTH

First discovered in Niger, West Africa, *Nigersaurus* (pronounced NAI-jer-SOR-us) was a Cretaceous-era lawn mower and vacuum cleaner in one. Its mouth was flat and wide—great for scooping up food—and filled with more than 500 replaceable teeth. No other animal on our planet has ever had a mower-mouth quite like this one! These specialized vegetarian jaws were perfectly adapted to graze on low-lying plants on the ground, just like those of a modern-day cow. *Nigersaurus* was small—at least for a sauropod—as it was only the size of an elephant compared to its whale-sized relatives. It also had a much shorter snout and neck than other sauropods, which helped it lunch on low-growing food.

MESOZOIC

| Triassic | Jurassic | Cretaceous |

10 Things to Spot

NAME GAME The first specimen ever studied was named *Nigersaurus taqueti*. *Nigersaurus*, the genus name, means reptile from the Niger.

FINE TOOTH COMB Nigersaur jaws looked like two sets of combs! Its teeth were packed in rows of around sixty in the front of the mouth. This dinosaur quickly wore down teeth while eating, and grew new teeth every two weeks.

TOOTHPICK TEETH *Nigersaurus* had 500 teeth—and more deep in their jaws ready to replace them! They were shaped like curved toothpicks. Together, these slender teeth formed a razor to slice up the dinosaur's favorite foods.

DUCK FACE The mouth on this sauropod was like a duck's beak, but blunt and flat in the front. The broad shape allowed it to suck up bits of food sheared off by its many, many teeth.

MOWER MOUTH Sauropods are known for having long necks. But some paleontologists believe the *Nigersaurus* could only slightly raise its neck, and nearly always held its head close to the ground like a lawn mower.

FEATHER WEIGHT The *Nigersaurus* skull was light due to large fenestrae, or openings, surrounded by very thin bone. The skull was still very strong and able to withstand the punishing stress of constant feeding.

FULL OF AIR Air sacs are holes in bone that decrease the weight of an animal. All sauropods had them, but the small Nigersaur had more air sacs than the average! Its vertebrae were full of air sacs that were attached to the lungs and filled them like balloons.

SMELL YOU LATER No one has found the nasal bones of a Nigersaur. Its nose was closer to its mouth than on other sauropods, and its nostrils were quite long. Skull scans suggest *Nigersaurus* had a weak sense of smell.

EYE SEE YOU The eyes of a Nigersaur were placed high on the sides of its head, giving it a nearly 360-degree view—like that of a cow. It needed a wide range of vision so it didn't become lunch while eating lunch!

CUTTING EDGE-OSAURUS Modern paleontologists take X-ray photos of fossils to see features that are invisible to the naked eye. Fragile *Nigersaurus* fossils were among the first ever to be studied in this way.

10 Things to Spot

 MISTAKEN IDENTITY In 1887, a skull fragment and two giant horns were attributed to an ancient bison! Further discoveries resolved this case of mistaken identity, and the "bison" was recognized as a *Triceratops*.

 BUILT LIKE A TANK Fossilized *Triceratops* skulls reaching lengths of nearly 9 feet have been found! These dinosaurs were built like tanks to hold up their heavy helmet-heads.

 LONG HORN The long horns on a *Triceratops*'s face would've been formidable defense against predators. Some fossils show scarring that suggests the horns were used in *Triceratops* tussles over territory and mates.

 CAPTIVATING KERATIN *Triceratops* frills were coved in keratin, a protein that makes hair, hooves, and horns. Their frills might have been brightly decorated to attract mates, declare dominance, and intimidate predators.

 ALL FRILLS Small triangular bones lined the edge of a *Triceratops* frill. These spikes gave extra protection to young dinosaurs, but flattened out with age.

 DINO ELDERS In 1891, skulls punctured with holes were discovered. The specimens were identified as a new species, *Torosaurus*. But some paleontologists think Torosaurs are just older *Triceratops* individuals. They believe that as a *Triceratops* aged, its frills lengthened, which opened holes in the skull.

 PRUNE FACE *Triceratops* had a narrow bird-like beak in front of its teeth. It was made of bone and was part of the dinosaur's skull. It worked like pruning shears to clip vegetation from shrubs, ferns, and other low-lying plants.

 SLOW GOOD *Triceratops* was twice the weight of an adult elephant, and could only run up to 20 mph. This might seem speedy, until you compare it to *Troodon*, which was likely able to achieve speeds up to 50 mph!

 FAMILY TIES All *Triceratops* fossils have been found alone except for three juveniles, and what appears to be a family group. Were adult *Triceratops* loners? Did they form temporary family groups? Research goes on.

 TO THE END *Triceratops* were among the last giants alive during the Age of Dinosaurs. They were so numerous before the Cretaceous extinction event that they're still the most commonly found Cretaceous dinosaurs in western North America!

MESOZOIC

| Triassic | Jurassic | Cretaceous |

10 THINGS TO SPOT

SKATEBOARD UNGUALS *Therizinosaurus* had three long unguals on each hand. The claws were about the same length as a skateboard, and they would've been intimidating!

SIDE SALAD *Therizinosaurus* claws had curved tips that wouldn't have been much use for digging or as weapons. So, what were they for? They were salad tongs to hook the branches of tall trees for a snack!

SIT-DOWN DINNER According to paleontologists, *Therizinosaurus* sat down to eat. Settled under a tree, it hooked branches for a sit-down dinner.

SPADE TEETH Paleontologists are yet to find *Therizinosaurus* teeth, but think its choppers were spade-shaped with serrated edges. This would've been perfect for stripping leaves off branches.

GO VEGGIE *Therizinosaurus* anatomy evolved to accommodate a vegetarian lifestyle. One of these changes was the development of a big pot belly, because a big stomach was needed to digest all of the plants they ate.

WATERWORLD *Therizinosaurus* lived in a forested landscape dotted by shallow lakes, mudflats, and meandering rivers. Amongst this wet environment, a favorite Therizinosaur meal was *Araucaria*, an ancient group of trees that survive today.

FIVE-TOED FEET *Therizinosaurus* walked on hind legs, just like humans! And like us, it had five toes on each foot, but only four were functional. The fifth toe was reduced to a nub, like the dewclaw on a cat.

CAPTIVATING CLAWS Many animals use oversized horns, antlers, tusks, and crests to attract a mate and intimidate rivals. It's possible *Therizinosaurus* used its unguals in a same way.

TURTLE TALONS When *Therizinosaurus* claws were discovered, paleontologists thought they belonged to a giant sea turtle. But later, the truth was discovered.

MET THEIR MATCH? *Therizinosaurus* were one of the largest dinosaurs in its habitat. Only the 10-foot tall *Tarbosaurus*, a relative of *T. rex*, could've been a predator, though we don't have direct evidence of a *Tarbosaurus* versus *Therizinosaurus* show-down.

17

QUITE THE CREST

The Late Cretaceous *Parasaurolophus* (pronounced pa-rah-SAW-ro-LOF-us) was a hadrosaur, one of the many types of duck-billed dinosaurs. Hadrosaurs earned this nickname due to the shapes of their mouths, although the *Parasaurolophus* mouth was more shovel-like than duck-like. This dinosaur likely roamed through large home territories in search of food. *Parasaurolophus* was a vegetarian and munched on leaves and twigs—and in particular, pine needles. Another distinguishing feature of hadrosaurs was the bony accessory on their heads: crests in a variety of shapes and sizes that looked a bit like party hats. The *Parasaurolophus* crest was one of the most impressive. The longest crest discovered so far is nearly 6 feet long!

MESOZOIC | Triassic | Jurassic | Cretaceous

10 Things to Spot

WE ARE FAMILY *Parasaurolophus* was a hadrosaur. This family included *Shantungosaurus*, the largest ever bipedal herbivorous dinosaur. Another, *Ajnabia*, would've barely reached the top of *Parasaurolophus*'s legs!

NOT THE SAME *Parasaurolophus* means "like *Saurolophus*." *Saurolophus* was a hadrosaur discovered before *Parasaurolophus*. The two looked similar, but turned out to be different.

A HEAD FOR FASHION Not all hadrosaurs had crests, but those that did modeled many styles. Some looked like shark fins and others like a unicorn's horn! *Parasaurolophus* had the longest crest of them all.

THREE OF A KIND There are three known species of *Parasaurolophus* based on variations in crest size and shape. It isn't easy to distinguish between them, though, as *Parasaurolophus* crests changed with age.

SNORKELSAURUS *Parasaurolophus* crests were hollow. This led some paleontologists to speculate that they were used as snorkels or air tanks, enabling the dinosaurs to forage underwater for aquatic plants.

TOTALLY COOL Crests might have helped regulate body temperature. Some paleontologists propose that warm blood flowed through vessels to the tip of the crest, releasing heat and cooling the body. This theory is still hotly debated.

INTO THE GROOVE Some illustrations of *Parasaurolophus* show a flap of skin connecting the long crest to the head. Grooves in fossils have been cited as evidence for this feature. No one knows for certain if the flap of skin existed.

MAKING MUSIC In the 1990s, scientists used computers to recreate the sound made by air forced through a *Parasaurolophus* crest. The result was a deep trumpeting sound!

EGG-CELLENT *Parasaurolophus* fossils have only been found in ancient floodplains, but they probably didn't live near water. It's believed that they lived in migrating herds and formed large nesting colonies where they laid their eggs.

ON THE HUNT *Parasaurolophus* found in Alberta, Canada, were hunted by two carnivorous species related to *T. rex*! They were called *Gorgosaurus* and *Daspletosaurus*, and they stalked primeval pine forests, seeming to split the hunting grounds between them.

10 Things to Spot

RANGE OF RAPTORS *Velociraptor* was a medium-sized dromaeosaurid. The largest were *Utahraptor* and *Austroraptor*. *Microraptor*, as the name suggests, was the smallest. It was the size of a big pigeon!

PREHISTORIC PEACOCK Dromaeosaurids had feathers that ranged from long decorative quills to warm fluff. The dinosaur was likely very colorful, and showed off its feathers to impress potential mates—just like a preening peacock.

AIRBORNE RAPTORS A *Velociraptor* relative called *Zhenyuanlong* was covered in feathers shaped like those used for flight. It couldn't fly, but it could probably glide.

SWIFT ROBBER *Velociraptor* was discovered in Mongolia. Its name means "swift robber," because the dinosaur was fast.

TOE-CURLING *Velociraptor* had four toes. Only two toes were used for walking, though. The others were a tiny dewclaw and the claw-toe, which were held off the ground.

RECURVED CLAWS The *Velociraptor* claw-toe was shaped like a sickle. When *Velociraptor* extended this toe, the claw would slash forward in a hooking motion.

REPTILE WRESTLING A fossil found in Mongolia showed a *Velociraptor*'s claws hooked on to a *Protoceratops*. It would've been a deadly wrestling match!

MOVIE MYTHS Raptors in movies use their claws to slice and dice their prey. Paleontologists think real-life raptors didn't do this. Their claws were the wrong shape and not strong enough to slash through the tough hide of larger animals.

UPHILL CLIMB Many paleontologists think *Velociraptor* claws were more like crampons or climbing hooks, used to grip large prey, while their teeth-filled jaws did the most damage.

BRAINIAC *Velociraptor* had one of the largest brains compared to its body size of any reptile. Because of this, some paleontologists think it was among the smartest dinos of the day.

WINGING IT

In 1861, the fossilized impression of a 150-million year old feather was uncovered in Germany. Its discovery shocked scientists because no one thought birds were that old. Since then, the feather has been linked to a fossilized reptile that had bird-like features such as feathered wings. *Archaeopteryx* (pronounced AR-key-OP-ter-icks), which means "ancient wing," was the name given to this extinct animal. It was a dinosaur *and* a bird. *Archaeopteryx* fossils and other discoveries have led paleontologists to conclude birds are dinosaurs. It's now known that many dinosaurs had feathers, but birds were the only dinosaurs to evolve wings and fly, and to survive the Cretaceous extinctions. Next time you feed ducks in the park, remember—you're feeding dinosaurs!

MESOZOIC		
Triassic	Jurassic	Cretaceous

SIZE COMPARISON

10 THINGS TO SPOT

 MISSING LINK *Archaeopteryx* had features of both modern birds and the dinosaurs it evolved from. But *Archaeopteryx* isn't the ancestor of modern birds. Paleontologists are still searching for this unknown relative.

 BIRD BODIES Fossilized bodies of twelve *Archaeopteryx* have been found. Many feature the outlines of feathers. These fossils have helped scientists piece together the evolution of birds from dinosaurs.

 FINE FEATHER The first *Archaeopteryx* feather was discovered in Solnhofen, Germany. During the Jurassic, this region was a shallow sea with small islands. Many fossils found here have been preserved in incredible detail.

 **LOW FLYER?** Unlike modern birds, *Archaeopteryx* didn't have a strong breastbone for wing muscles to attach to the body. This suggests it wasn't a good flyer. Some scientists think it couldn't do more than glide.

 FEATHER TROUSERS Fossilized hindleg feathers of *Archaeopteryx* have been found. They would've looked like fluffy sweatpants worn by the birds to stay warm.

 PERFECT BALANCE An *Archaeopteryx* tail was made of bone. Feathers grew from it like leaves on a branch. The tail was very stiff and would've increased balance while running and during flight.

 BALD HEADED? There's no fossil evidence of feathers on an *Archaeopteryx*'s head. Was this bird bald like a vulture? Probably not. Paleontologists think its feathers tended to fall off before fossilization could occur.

 NEVERMORE Scientists determined *Archaeopteryx* was black like a raven. Another study concluded it was black and white. We might never know the actual color of *Archaeopteryx*.

 **WING CLAWS** *Archaeopteryx* had many features lost in most modern birds. One of these is three clawed fingers on the wings. The claws might have been used to climb trees. As they were carnivores, the claws also could've been used to seize and pin down prey.

 SICKLE CLAWS *Archaeopteryx* had an extendable sickle claw on each foot, just like its relative, the *Velociraptor*. Whereas *Velociraptor* wielded its sickle claws like knives while hunting, we're not sure how *Archaeopteryx* used its claws. They could've held down prey or aided in climbing.

SPINNING PLATES

Stegosaurus (pronounced STE-go-SOR-us) is iconic. With distinctive plates on its back, this herbivore ranks among the most well-known dinosaurs. Exactly how the plates were positioned and what they were used for, however, is still a mystery. The discovery of *Stegosaurus* fossils by O.C. Marsh fueled a fossil frenzy. The rush to find fossils was so intense that we call this period the Bone Wars! O.C. Marsh and his rival E.D. Cope turned to theft, lies, and trickery to be the first to describe new species. Their fossil feud led to the identification of 136 new dinosaurs—but also to their downfalls. Years of underhanded schemes drained their bank accounts and destroyed their reputations as scientists.

MESOZOIC

Triassic | Jurassic | Cretaceous

10 THINGS TO SPOT

 PLENTY OF PLATES *Stegosaurus* is known for the sail-like plates on its back. Different stegosaur species sported different plate shapes. Some were rounded and others were spiky.

 PROTECTIVE PLATES *Stegosaurus* plates might have been used as protective armor. But some studies have shown that the plates were too weak to be effective against a predator's powerful jaws.

 DINO AIR-CON Another theory links *Stegosaurus* plates to thermoregulation. But some stegosaurs had spike-like plates that wouldn't have been much use as air conditioners. Studies continue . . .

 DRESS TO IMPRESS *Stegosaurus* plates were probably colorfully patterned. If so, they would've displayed them to demonstrate strength. The flashier, the better!

 PUZZLING POSITION The position of *Stegosaurus* plates is a puzzle! O.C. Marsh thought they laid flat like a turtle shell, then later thought they were a single row of standing plates. Today, most agree the plates formed two staggered rows down the back.

 RAINBOW BACKS *Stegosaurus* hind legs are twice the height of their forelimbs. Because of this, paleontologists once thought they were bipedal. We now know *Stegosaurus* walked on all-fours. Its back and tail curved like a rainbow!

 BUNCH OF BONES The most complete *Stegosaurus* fossil is named Sophie. She was named after the daughter of a man who helped the Natural History Museum in London buy the dinosaur for their collection.

 TINY BRAIN Compared to its body size, *Stegosaurus*'s head was tiny. Its brain was about the size of a lime! Our spiky-tailed friend wasn't the cleverest of creatures, but nevertheless, the family survived for nearly 100 million years.

 HOLEY MOLEY *Stegosaurus* could protect itself against *Allosaurus*. It had a strong tail armed with long spikes. A fossilized *Allosaurus* bone is evidence of a Jurassic showdown. It has a hole in it the same size as a *Stegosaurus* tail spike!

 STEGOSAURUS STEAK The therapod *Allosaurus* was a top predator of the Late Jurassic. A *Stegosaurus* neck plate found in Utah has a bite mark that matches the shape of an *Allosaurus* jaw!

WELCOME TO THE CLUB

In 1906, the first *Ankylosaurus* (pronounced an-KAI-low-SOR-us) fossils were discovered in a fossil-rich region called the Hell Creek Formation in Montana. Because so few of its bones were discovered, early reconstructions showed *Ankylosaurus* as a stegosaur-like dinosaur without back plates. The defining feature of this herbivorous dinosaur was a tail that ended in a semi-circular club the size of a human head! Only one *Ankylosaurus* club has ever been found, although the fossilized clubs from close relatives have been studied. Paleontologists speculate that clubs probably got bigger with age, and that the tails of male animals were larger than the tails of females. *Ankylosaurus* means "stiff lizard" in reference to the bones fused stiffly together to make this bulky, solid animal.

MESOZOIC | Triassic | Jurassic | Cretaceous

10 THINGS TO SPOT

 SWING IT The club tail of an *Ankylosaurus* was a powerful defense against predators. The force from the swinging tail would've been able to crush bone like a giant sledgehammer!

 CLUB-TAIL COMBAT Club tails might have had another purpose: fighting. Fossils of *Ankylosaurus* relatives have damage that matches a club-tail strike. It's possible ankylosaurs wielded their tails in combats over territory, food, mates—or all of the above!

 SOFT SPOT The osteoderms that covered an *Ankylosaurus*'s head and back formed an impenetrable suit of armor. But the dinosaur's belly was softer. It was a weak spot they might have protected by lying flat on the ground when threatened.

 **ORNATE OSTEODERMS** *Ankylosaurus* osteoderms formed rows of thick, protective structures called scutes. Some ankylosaur scutes grew into thorn-shaped spikes all over their bodies. Some scute spikes were even longer than their heads!

 HEAD HORNS *Ankylosaurus* had two backward-pointing horns behind each eye. These spikes would've offered additional protection for the head and could've been used as weapons against predators.

 ARMORED COLLARS Even the neck was armored on an *Ankylosaurus*! Arcs of bone protected this vulnerable area like a tough neck-brace.

 BIG AND SLOW *Ankylosaurus* was heavy and slow. With all of those osteoderms and that massive clubbed tail, predators probably didn't bother facing down a full-grown individual!

 DIG IT! Some paleontologists think ankylosaur was a digger! A fossil found in Mongolia had limbs suited for digging. Plus, the nostrils of *Ankylosaurus* faced sideways—another possible adaptation for digging.

 FRUIT FLAVORS Studies of *Ankylosaurus* teeth and jaws suggest it ate soft foods like leaves and fruit. If this dinosaur was a digger, it could've included a side of tubers and roots with their fruit salad snacks.

 GULP! *Ankylosaurus* had more teeth than any of its relatives. Its teeth were suited to cropping soft vegetation, which was then swallowed whole. There's no evidence *Ankylosaurus* chewed its food!

A NECK AHEAD

Diplodocus (pronounced dih-PLOD-oh-cus) was a sauropod, a type of dinosaur that grew to enormous size, and were the largest creatures to ever walk Earth! *Diplodocus* wasn't even the biggest sauropod, but it was one of the longest. The neck of an adult was longer than the body. The whip-like tail was more than three times the body length. Like all sauropods, *Diplodocus* was an herbivore. It shared a grassy, lightly wooded habitat with a variety of animals, including predators like *Allosaurus* and *Ceratosaurus*. A full-grown *Diplodocus* likely had little to fear from these much smaller theropods, though. Size was one of *Diplodocus*'s most effective defenses.

10 THINGS TO SPOT

 SNAKE TAIL The dinosaur had about eighty tail bones—almost double the number of other sauropods! The tail tapered into a thin, flexible, snake-like tip.

 CRACK THAT WHIP Some paleontologists think *Diplodocus* used its tail like a whip as a defensive weapon. Another theory suggests the dinosaur cracked that whip to communicate across vast distances.

 HERD MENTALITY *Diplodocus* were herd animals that traveled in large groups. Their long tails could've functioned like feelers, sensing the position of neighboring *Diplodocus* and helping to keep the herd together.

 BALANCING ACT Another use for *Diplodocus*'s tail was to balance its long, heavy neck. The bones in the mid-section of the tail had paired beam-like structures. This feature gives *Diplodocus* its name, which means, "double beam."

 NECK WARS *Diplodocus* necks might have been weapons! Modern giraffes swing their necks at rivals during courtship battles. Paleontologists think adult *Diplodocus* males might have engaged in similar behavior.

 BLOWHOLE MYSTERY *Diplodocus*'s skull has large openings on the forehead. Scientists once thought these were like the blowhole of a whale—and that *Diplodocus* was aquatic! This dinosaur might have enjoyed the occasional dip, but they were much more comfortable on land.

 LEAF LOVER *Diplodocus* wasn't a fussy eater. It'd chomp down on a branch and swallow the leaves by stripping them off with peg-like teeth in the front of the mouth.

 REACH UP *Diplodocus* walked on all fours. But to reach the highest trees, it didn't raise its head—it reared up on its strong hind legs!

 STRIKE! Two types of *Diplodocus* are recognized by most paleontologists. *Diplodocus carnegii* is the smaller of the two. The larger species, *Diplodocus hallorum*, was almost as long as a bowling lane!

 **CELEBRITY DIPPY** The most famous *Diplodocus* is named Dippy. It's a model made from the fossils of several different individuals and related species. The original skeleton is at the Carnegie Museum of Natural History. Copies were made for museums all around the world.

29

SET SAIL!

Many animals have sails on their backs, like the crested chameleon from Central Africa, which displays a small crest that can change color along with the rest of its body. But no animal has ever had a sail as spectacular as that of the *Spinosaurus* (pronounced SPY-no-SOR-us). The structure was taller than most full-grown humans and about twice as long! The first *Spinosaurus* fossil, which included some teeth, skull fragments, and bony spines from the sail, was discovered in Egypt in 1912. But the fossil was completely destroyed during World War II. Luckily, a handful of images and descriptions created by scientists survived. In the next one hundred years, several more *Spinosaurus* fossil discoveries would reveal a dinosaur that is still the longest land carnivore ever and the only dinosaur we know of who lived in water!

SIZE COMPARISON

MESOZOIC

Triassic | Jurassic | Cretaceous

10 THINGS TO SPOT

 SPINY LIZARD Ernst Stromer was the paleontologist who named *Spinosaurus*. Its full name, *Spinosaurus aegyptiacus*, means "Egyptian spined lizard," a nod to the country where the dinosaur was found.

 T. REX WANNABE Stromer knew *Spinosaurus* was a theropod—and that the fossil spines supported a sail on the dinosaur's back. But he assumed *Spinosaurus* was bipedal like most theropods, and illustrated the dinosaur as a *T. rex* with a sail.

 GONE FISHIN' *Spinosaurus* was bipedal, but it didn't stand up like a *T. rex*. *Spinosaurus* had a hunched posture while it walked. Its clawed hands were free to scratch an itch or catch fish.

 ALL-PURPOSE SAIL The sail might have been a brightly colored accessory to attract mates and intimidate rivals. It also might have been used in thermoregulation.

 SINK OR SWIM *Spinosaurus* lived—at least part of the time—in water. Its body shape is similar to that of the sail fish, which has sails that aid it in swimming. Whether *Spinosaurus* was a strong swimmer or more at home in the shallow end is still debated.

 BUILT-IN OAR A *Spinosaurus*'s tail was flattened sideways like an oar. The tail also had a small crest. Both of these features would've made the tail a great adaptation for swimming!

 CROC FACE A *Spinosaurus*'s nostrils were near the top of its head. It would've been able to breathe as long as its nostrils were above water. It's a feature this dinosaur shared with crocodiles.

 WEBBED FEET *Spinosaurus* feet looked like the feet of shorebirds that walk on sandy, wet ground. Some paleontologists think *Spinosaurus* might have had webbed hind feet for swimming!

 SOMETHING FISHY The fossilized *Spinosaurus* jaw discovered in Egypt was long and squared off at the tip—again, like a crocodile. The teeth were cone-shaped instead of serrated. These are all characteristics of a fish-loving dinosaur.

 LAST MEAL *Spinosaurus* didn't just eat fish. Fossils of the closely related *Baryonyx* contained fish scales and the bones of a young *Iguanodon* in its stomach. The bone of a flying reptile called a pterosaur was found with a spinosaur tooth stuck on it!

31

BONE HEAD

The dome head of the *Pachycephalosaurus* (pronounced pack-ee-SEF-a-low-SOR-us) made it a formidable dinosaur. Its name means "thick-headed lizard"—and its head was really thick! Its skull was built like a battering ram and might have been used to fight off rivals, impress potential mates, and warn off predators. Bony bumps and spikes surrounded the solid head, and they varied quite a bit between species and even between individuals. Some paleontologists have proposed that the differences might have been used by *Pachycephalosaurus* to tell each other apart, the way we do with faces. This herbivorous dinosaur was a species that lived at the very end of the Cretaceous, and would've witnessed the last days of the Age of Dinosaurs.

MESOZOIC | Triassic | Jurassic | Cretaceous

SIZE COMPARISON

10 THINGS TO SPOT

A HEAD FOR COMPUTING No animal has a skull quite like the bone-headed *Pachycephalosaurus*. The domed top can be up to 9 inches thick. That's the height of an average laptop screen!

HEADACHES Studies of pachycephalosaur fossils revealed that 22% had head injuries. Scientists also found traces of specialized cells that sped up healing. This is evidence that these dinosaurs used their heads to fight each other.

CURVED NECK *Pachycephalosaurus* necks were curved. Many paleontologists think they couldn't have headbutted each other because their necks weren't built to take head-on blows.

WRECKING BALL An alternative to headbutting is flank-butting. Rival *Pachycephalosaurus* might have fought each other by swinging their heads like wrecking balls. Their skulls would strike the opponent's flank, or side, which minimized serious injuries.

ANCIENT ARMADILLO The first *Pachycephalosaurus* found was thought to be the armor of an extinct armadillo! Over one hundred years later, the fossil was finally recognized as a fragment from a dinosaur skull.

WIZARD LIZARD In 2004, a pachycephalosaur fossil that looked like a dragon's skull was discovered. It was named *Dracorex hogwartsia* or "Hogwarts dragon king," a reference to the magical school from the *Harry Potter* series.

PACHYCEPHALOSAUR PUPS? *Stygimoloch* was another pachycephalosaur with a dragon-like skull. It was relatively flat and covered with spiky horns. Some paleontologists think *Stygimoloch* and *Dracorex* were young *Pachycephalosaurus*.

WAIT FOR IT A dragon-headed pachycephalosaur was discovered in South Dakota. Named Sandy after the location where it was found, it was thought to be an adult. Paleontologists are waiting patiently for breaking news from scientists studying this dinosaur.

EYE SEE YOU *Pachycephalosaurus* had binocular vision, with eyes that faced forward. This is unusual for prey animals, who usually have eyes on the sides of their heads so they can see all around them and spot predators.

SAY CHEESE Some paleontologists think *Pachycephalosaurus* was omnivorous. Its small, blade-like teeth and binocular vision suggest it might have added a side order of meat to a mostly vegetarian diet.

A BIT PRICKLY

Amargasaurus (pronounced ah-MAR-gah-SOR-us) was a relative of *Diplodocus*. It was small for a sauropod, reaching only 42 feet in length. What made this herbivorous dinosaur really stand out were the huge rows of spines that stuck out from its neck. They looked like over-sized combs with the teeth facing up! The longest spines discovered so far were almost 2 feet in length. That's about the same height as a golden retriever. The spines curved backward in a dome-like shape and prevented the dinosaur from raising its neck. Because of this, along with its short neck, paleontologists believe *Amargasaurus* fed on smaller plants that were within easy reach.

SIZE COMPARISON

10 Things to Spot

 ARGENTINIAN DINOSAUR A big collection of *Amargasaurus* bones were excavated in Argentina. The sauropod gets its name from the La Amarga formation fossil bed, where it was found.

 BENDING BACKWARD *Amargasaurus* neck spikes stuck out from the skin and curved backward. There were two rows of spikes that began just after the head and ended before the back.

 **SPIKY DEFENCE** Neck spikes on an *Amargasaurus* were likely covered in keratin. This would've made the spikes up to twice as long and very strong. Biting this dinosaur would've been like chomping a pin cushion!

 **SWORDPLAY** *Amargasaurus* might have wielded its neck spikes like swords. Bending its neck backward, the spikes could've pierced attackers lurking from behind. Bend the neck down, and . . . en garde! The spikes would've created two impenetrable columns of swords.

 MAKING MUSIC Some studies suggest that *Amargasaurus* neck spikes were musical, and would've sounded like drumsticks when struck together! These dinosaurs might have tapped tunes to attract mates, warn off rivals, or send messages to each other.

 HOLD IT UP Not everyone thinks *Amargasaurus* had a spiky neck. Some think its spikes were a scaffold for skin that formed a sail-like crest. Most pro-crest scientists believe that one sail covered both rows of spikes.

 BIG BALLOON If *Amargasaurus* had a giant crest, it might have been used as an air sac! Some paleontologists think it was filled with air like a big balloon, and connected to the lungs to help the large animal breathe.

 WHICH PATTERN? What color was *Amargasaurus*'s sail? No one knows for sure. It could've been very colorful with vibrant patterns like spots or stripes!

 BISON-LIKE The vertebrae on an *Amargasaurus* had bumps. Paleontologists think the bumps were covered by skin, and gave this sauropod a fleshy hump over its back and hips, like modern-day bison.

 CROC CROSSING There's no direct fossil evidence of predators that hunted *Amargasaurus*. The crocodile-like reptile named *Amargasuchus* is a strong contender. The two animals were named after the same fossil bed. They shared the same habitat and likely crossed paths.

35

10 Things to Spot

RIVER RUN The full name of this creature is *Kulindadromeus zabaikalicus*. *Kulindadromeus* means "Kulinda River running dinosaur" to honor the river near where it was discovered. *Zabaikalicus* honors the Zabaykalsky Krai, the Siberian region where the dinosaur was found.

FORTUNATE FIND Fossils from the Ukurey Formation fossil bed in Siberia were formed by fine volcanic ash, which preserved even the tiniest of features. If *Kulindadromeus* hadn't lived in this area, we might not have known about its feathers!

SPUR SCALES *Kulindadromeus* had three types of scales. Overlapping hexagons covered its lower shins. The hands, feet and ankles had small round scales. The tail featured five rows of large rectangular scales that had overlapping spurs, creating an armor-like pattern.

REPTILE RIBBONS *Kulindadromeus* was the oldest feathered dinosaur. It had three feather types. Fuzz covered its body, neck, and head. On the upper arm and thigh were string-like feathers. The unique feathers on its lower legs looked like bundles of ribbons!

GROUNDED FOR LIFE *Kulindadromeus* couldn't fly. It didn't have wings, and its feathers weren't shaped the right way. Flight feathers are very different from the ribbon-like feathers on *Kulindadromeus*.

DINOSAUR DATING Feathers likely evolved to keep dinosaurs warm. The fuzz on a *Kulindadromeus* was like a sweater. It was probably brightly colored for courtship and territory displays.

CHEW ON THIS *Kulindadromeus* was a herbivore. What makes this dinosaur's eating habits unusual is that it chewed its food. Most dinosaurs swallowed their meals whole!

HIDE & SEEK This small, bipedal dinosaur didn't have armor—no club-tail or spikes. The only trick up *Kulindadromeus*'s sleeve was to run away! It was quick and agile, able to hide in small spaces to avoid predators.

SNACK TIME! The only evidence of a predator that might have hunted *Kulindadromeus* is a tooth. Paleontologists think it might have belonged to an *Allosaurus*-like theropod that had *Kulindadromeus* for a snack.

SENSITIVE DETECTORS The shape of *Kulindadromeus*'s skull suggests it had good eyesight, hearing, and sense of smell. These would have come in handy to detect predators before getting away fast.

THE AGE OF DINOSAURS

Now that you've seen all of the dinosaurs in the book, check out when they lived and how big they were compared to each other—and to us humans!

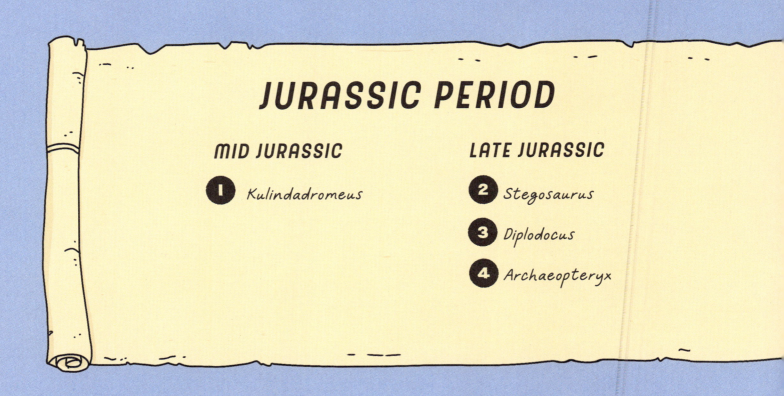

JURASSIC PERIOD

MID JURASSIC
1. Kulindadromeus

LATE JURASSIC
2. Stegosaurus
3. Diplodocus
4. Archaeopteryx

CRETACEOUS PERIOD

EARLY CRETACEOUS
- **5** Amargasaurus

MID CRETACEOUS
- **6** Nigersaurus

LATE CRETACEOUS
- **7** Spinosaurus
- **8** Parasaurolophus
- **9** Therizinosaurus
- **10** Velociraptor
- **11** Pachycephalosaurus
- **12** Ankylosaurus
- **13** Triceratops
- **14** T. rex

TIMELINE OF DISCOVERIES

PACHYCEPHALOSAURUS
Found in Lance Formation, Montana, USA
Discovered c. 1860

ARCHAEOPTERYX
Found in Solnhofen Limestone Formation, Solnhofen, Germany
Discovered in 1861

PARASAUROLOPHUS
Found in Dinosaur Park Formation, Alberta, Canada
Discovered in 1922

SPINOSAURUS
Found in the Bahariya Formation, Western Desert, Egypt
Discovered in 1912

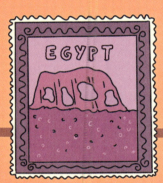

VELOCIRAPTOR
Found in Flaming Cliffs, Gobi Desert, Mongolia
Discovered in 1923

THERIZINOSAURUS
Found in Nemeget Formation, Gobi Desert, Mongolia
Discovered in 1948

NIGERSAURUS
Found in Elrhaz Formation, Gadoufaoua, Niger
Discovered 1956-72, described 1976

40

STEGOSAURUS
Found in YPM Quarry,
Colorado, USA
Discovered in 1877

DIPLODOCUS
Found in the Marshall P. Felch Quarry,
Colorado, USA
Discovered in 1877

TRICERATOPS
Found in Denver, Colorado, USA
Discovered in 1887

ANKYLOSAURUS
Found in Hell Creek Formation, Montana, USA
Discovered in 1906

T. REX
Found in South Table Mountain,
Colorado, USA
Discovered in 1902

AMARGASAURUS
Found in La Amarga, Neuquen Province
of northern Patagonia
Discovered in 1984

KULINDADROMEUS
Found in Ukureyskaya Formation,
Zabaykalsky Krai region of Siberia
Described in 2014

ANSWERS

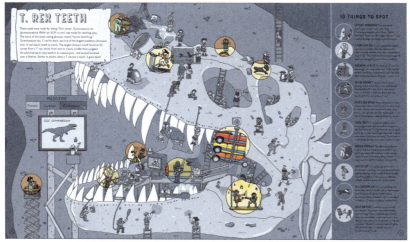

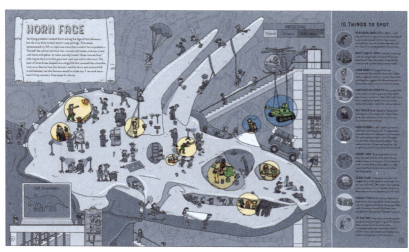
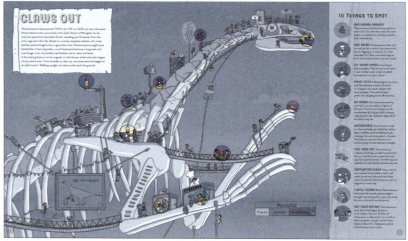
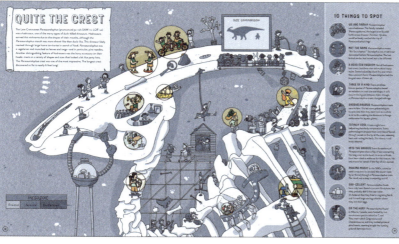

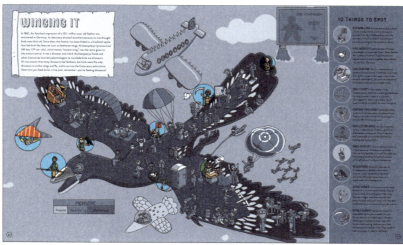

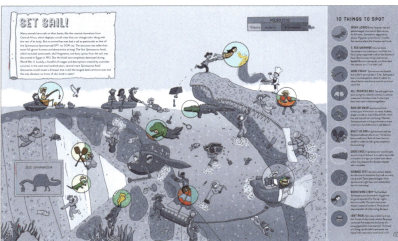
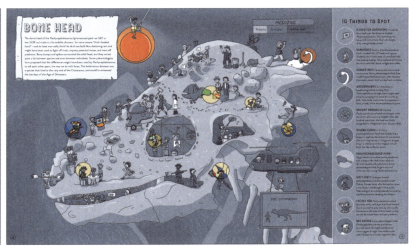
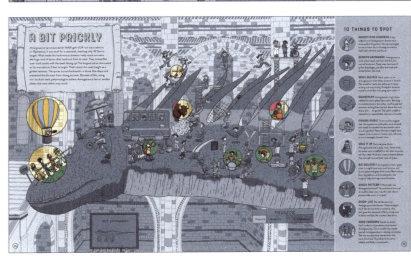

43

GLOSSARY

ADAPTATION a process in which a living thing slowly changes over time to better suit its habitat.

AIR SACS holes in bones that decrease the weight of an animal.

ANATOMY the structure of a plant or animal.

BIPEDAL an animal that walks on two legs.

CARNIVOROUS a diet that consists of mainly eating other animals.

CERATOPSIAN a group of herbivorous dinosaurs that had a frilled bone on the back of their skulls and parrot-like beaks.

CHARACTERISTIC a feature that can be used to identify someone or something.

CONVERGENT EVOLUTION a process in which unrelated animals evolve similar characteristics.

CREST a ridge of feathers, fur, or skin on the head or neck of an animal.

CRETACEOUS a period of time that began 145 million years ago, and lasted for about 80 million years.

CRETACEOUS EXTINCTION an extinction event that occurred at the end of the Cretaceous Period that wiped out nearly 80% of life.

DEWCLAW a small toe that has almost disappeared.

EVOLVE to change over a period of time due to pressures from the environment.

FENESTRAE natural holes or openings in a bone.

FLOODPLAINS flat land next to a river or stream that is often underwater.

FOSSIL the preserved remains or traces of a plant or animal that lived a long time ago.

GENUS NAME a name given to a group of living things that are very closely related.

GPS Global Positioning System: a network of devices in space that send signals to Earth, and can help pinpoint the position of a place.

HABITAT a place in which a plant or animal lives.

HADROSAUR a group of dinosaurs that had snouts that looked like duck bills.

HATCHLING an animal that has recently hatched from an egg.

HERBIVOROUS a diet that consists of eating plants.

IMPRESSION a fossilized imprint or mold, such as a footprint.

JURASSIC a period of time that began 201 million years ago, and lasted for about 56 million years.

KERATIN a natural material that forms body features like hair, fur, feathers, nails, hooves, and horns.

MATRIX the natural material, such as rock or clay, that something is embedded in.

MUDFLAT a flat area underwater that becomes exposed when the tide goes out.

OMNIVOROUS a diet that consists of eating both plants and animals.

OSTEODERM a bony material in the skin of some animals that can form scales, plates, and armor.

PALEONTOLOGIST a scientist who studies ancient life.

PETRIFIED the remains of a plant or animal that has been turned to stone. It's a process that takes millions of years.

PLATE a flat, hard piece of bone or horn that protects the body of an animal.

PLUME a decorative feather or collection of feathers on the body of a bird.

PREDATOR a living creature that hunts other life forms for food.

PREHISTORIC the time in history before written records.

PREY a living creature that is hunted by others for food.

PROTEIN the building blocks for life on Earth.

QUILL the flight feather of a bird.

REPTILE a type of animal that has a spine, is generally cold-blooded, and usually lays eggs on land, like a snake or a crocodile.

SAIL a large, mostly flat growth on an animal's back that often grows out of bones in its vertebrae.

SAUROPOD a group of large herbivorous dinosaurs that had a long neck and tail, and walked on four legs.

SCUTE a thick plate made of bone or horn.

SEDIMENT material, such as soil or sand, desposited by natural forces like wind and water.

SERRATED something that has a jagged edge.

SICKLE a tool with a curved blade.

SPECIES a group of closely related living things.

SPECIMEN a plant or animal that is an example of its species.

TERRITORY an area of land frequented and defended by an animal.

THERMOREGULATION the natural processes that help a living thing maintain its temperature.

THEROPODS a group of carnivorous dinosaurs that walked on two legs.

TRIASSIC a period of time that began 252 million years ago, and lasted for about 50 million years.

UNGUAL a toe that ends with a claw, hoof, or nail.

VERTEBRAE the bones that make up the spine of an animal.

VESSELS a network of tubes that move fluids around inside the body of a living thing.

WOULD YOU LIKE TO DELVE EVEN DEEPER INTO THE PREHISTORIC WORLD? LOOK OUT FOR THESE BOOKS ON DINOSAURS.

Illumisaurus by Lucy Brownridge and Carnovsky (Wide Eyed Editions, 2020)

When Dinosaurs Conquered the Skies by Jingmai O'Connor and Maria Brzozowska (words & pictures, 2022)

Dictionary of Dinosaurs by Dr. Matthew G. Baron and Dieter Braun (Wide Eyed Editions, 2024)

The Story of Dinosaurs by Catherine Barr, Steve Williams and Amy Husband
(Frances Lincoln Children's Books, 2024)

Oh No They Aren't: Nature by Eric Huang and Sam Caldwell (words & pictures, 2025)